THE GUYS' GUIDE TO MAKING CITY LIFE MORE AWESOME

BY ERIC BRAUN

CAPSTONE PRESS

a capstone imprint

Edge Books are published by Capstone Press,
1710 Roe Crest Drive, North Mankato, Minnesota 56003
www.capstonepub.com

Library of Congress Cataloging-in-Publication Data
Braun, Eric, 1971–
The guys' guide to making city life more awesome / by Eric Braun.
pages cm.—(Edge books. The guys' guides)
Includes bibliographical references and index.
Summary: "Describes various tips, activities, and useful information for making life
in the city more fun and interesting"—Provided by publisher.
ISBN 978-1-4765-3923-2 (library binding)
ISBN 978-1-4765-5971-1 (eBook PDF)
1. City and town life—Juvenile literature. I. Title.
HT152.B73 2014
307.76—dc23   2013035404

Editorial Credits
Aaron Sautter, editor; Veronica Scott, designer; Eric Gohl, media researcher;
Jennifer Walker, production specialist

Photo Credits
Alamy: tbkmedia.de, 16 (bottom); Capstone: 6; Capstone Studio: Karon Dubke, 7;
Dreamstime: Linda Morland, 17 (bottom), Rolf52, 28 (bottom left), Sean Pavone,
11 (top), Thomas Vieth, 20, Valentin Armianu, 29 (top); Getty Images: AFP/Denis
Charlet, 11 (middle), European School, 26 (middle), Flickr Vision/John Dillon, 19
(top), SSPL, 11 (bottom); Newscom: Everett Collection, 26 (bottom), Mirrorpix/
Daily Mirror, 28 (bottom right); Shutterstock: 1973kla, 2, Anikakodydkova, 24
(middle), Bikeworldtravel, 10 (top), cristapper, 9 (top right), Danussa, cover, 10–11
(background), 18–19 (background), 22–23 (background), 24–25 (background),
digidreamgrafix, 23 (middle), Dmitry Naumov, 23 (bottom), Eric Broder Van Dyke,
9 (top left), Eric Isselee, 26 (top), Fernando Cortes, 9 (bottom right), hin255, 14 (top),
hxdyl, 28 (middle), Jacek Chabraszewski, 24 (bottom), jennyt, 15 (top), Jun Mu, 13
(bottom), Leonard Zhukovsky, 10 (bottom), littleny, 21 (bottom), MaKars, 13 (top),
Marie C Fields, 28 (top), MARKABOND, 23 (top), Matt Knoth, 12, Mayovskyy
Andrew, 17 (top right), Migel, 25, Mihai-Bogdan Lazar, 17 (top left), Monkey
Business Images, 24 (top), Naira Kalantaryan, 16 (top), Petr Jilek, 15 (bottom),
PRILL, 21 (top), Radu Bercan, 9 (bottom left), Rahhal, 29 (middle), Sandy Stupart,
8 (left), Scotshot, 18, Spirit of America, 19 (middle), Stuart Monk, 29 (bottom), Tony
Campbell, 14 (bottom), Tupungato, 4–5, Visun Khankasem, 19 (bottom), WDG Photo,
8 (right), Zlatko Guzmic, 7 (background), 21 (background)

Design Elements: Shutterstock

Printed in the United States of America in Stevens Point, Wisconsin.
092013   007768WZS14

TABLE OF CONTENTS

FUN CITY LIVING

Your bus stops with a mechanical sigh. When you step onto the busy street, you hear honking car horns and thumping car stereos. Maybe you smell hot dogs, popcorn, or Chinese food from nearby food carts. What do you want to do? You can go see the newest movie or check out a cool book store. You could also visit a museum, hang out at a beautiful park, and much more. Your options are wide open—this is a busy city!

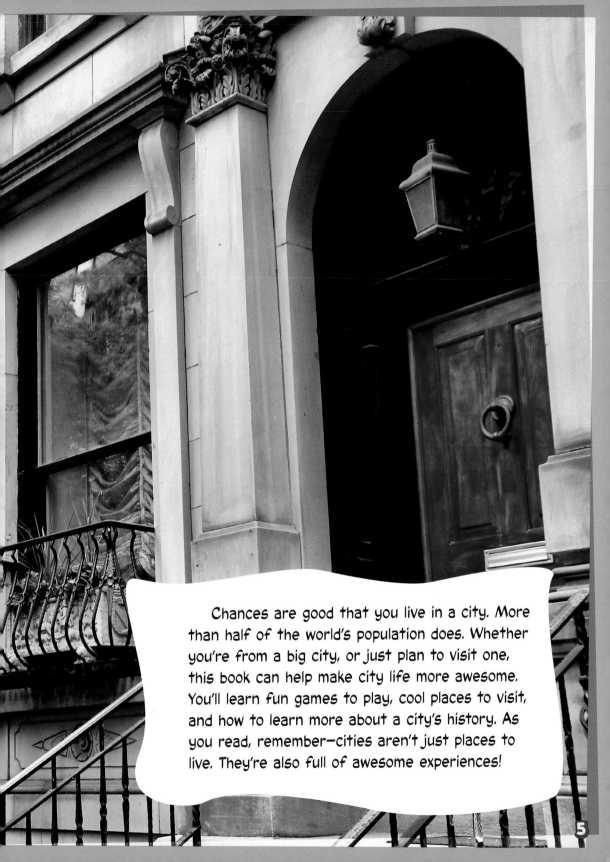

Chances are good that you live in a city. More than half of the world's population does. Whether you're from a big city, or just plan to visit one, this book can help make city life more awesome. You'll learn fun games to play, cool places to visit, and how to learn more about a city's history. As you read, remember—cities aren't just places to live. They're also full of awesome experiences!

PLAY FUN CITY GAMES

Many sports need a lot of open space, which isn't always available in the city. But some sports can be played in smaller spaces such as front yards or school playgrounds. Gather your friends and have some fun trying out the following neighborhood games.

CAPTURE THE FLAG

You can play this action-packed game across yards or in an alley. You need two teams, each with its own territory. Each team hides a flag or treasure in its territory. Players cross into their opponents' area to try to find the flag and take it safely to their own side. When on the opponents' side, you can be tagged and sent to their "jail" at the back of their territory. Players can rescue jailed teammates by tagging them. The first team to carry the opposing team's flag to their own side wins.

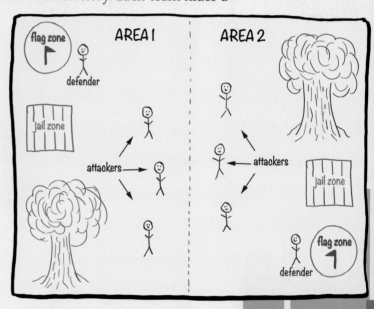

TIP: Capture the flag is perfect for neighborhoods with lots of hiding places like trees, bushes, fences, or small sheds. Before you start, create a game plan with your team. Decide who will distract the other team, who will go after the opposing flag, and who will stay to defend your team's flag.

KICK THE CAN

Guys have been playing this city classic for generations. Maybe your father or grandfather played it! Kick the can is similar to hide-and-seek. You'll need a metal can and at least four players.

1. Find an open area to play and set aside some space for a "jail." Set boundaries so players don't just run to the next block. Then decide which player will be "It."

2. The "It" player places the can in the center of the play area. He then counts out loud to 100 while the other players hide.

3. After counting, the "It" player looks for the hiders. If one is found, he points to the hider and calls out his name. Then both players race back to the can.

4. If "It" gets to the can first, the hider goes to jail. But if the hider gets there first, he kicks the can hard and calls out, "All ye, all ye, out and free!" Anyone in jail is then set free and runs to hide again. The "It" player then has to pick up the can and place it back in the center.

5. If the "It" player sends everyone to jail, the first hider who was caught becomes the new "It" player.

GO ON A PHOTO SCAVENGER HUNT

Cities are loaded with cool sights to see. Why not gather some buddies and explore your city by going on a photo scavenger hunt? Each person gets a digital camera and a list of items to photograph. Then set a time limit and start taking pictures. You can work alone or in teams of two or three. Whoever gets the most photos on the list wins. Here are some suggestions to get you started:

A STATUE

AN ELECTRIC SIGN

A FOUNTAIN

SOMETHING THAT HAS BEEN SPILLED

A CAR WITH A VANITY LICENSE PLATE

A TEAMMATE CLIMBING A TREE

A SIDEWALK SIGNBOARD

A FLOWERING PLANT

TIP:

You can make your scavenger hunt "green" by collecting trash as you go. Players can get bonus points for picking up plastic bottles, foam cups, or other trash.

A POLICE CAR OR FIRE TRUCK

A BUILDING WITH STONE COLUMNS

A CONSTRUCTION SITE

A TICKET BOOTH AT A SPORTS STADIUM OR THEATER

YOURSELF REFLECTED IN A MIRROR

A BIRD NEST ON A BUILDING

AWESOME WAYS TO GET AROUND IN CITIES

Many people get around cities in cars or buses. But some cities offer other cool forms of transportation. If you're in a big city, try out one of the following ways to get from place to place.

SUBWAYS

People in cars often get stuck in traffic jams. But **subways** can zoom along nonstop powered by up to 625 volts of electricity! London had the world's first underground railway, which opened in 1863. Although its nickname is "the Tube," more than half of the Underground's tracks are actually above ground.

The New York City subway is another famous system. When it opened in 1904, it had 9 miles (14.5 kilometers) of track. Today New York's subway system has 660 miles (1,062 km) of track and carries 5.4 million riders each weekday.

PUBLIC BIKES

Many cities have a system for renting or sharing bicycles. Bike stations are set up throughout the city. People check out a bike at one station, ride it where they need to go, and then check it in at another station. China has the world's largest bike sharing program, called the Hangzhou Public Bicycle Program. Several other cities have similar programs, including the Vélib' system in Paris, France, CitiRide in New York, and Nice Ride in Minneapolis, Minnesota.

AWESOME TRAVEL BETWEEN CITIES

There are some awesome ways people can travel from one city to another as well. Here are a couple incredible ways people travel between cities and countries in some parts of the world.

THE SHINKANSEN

The Shinkansen inter-city rail line in Japan is nicknamed the "Bullet Train." It moves people between Japan's two main islands at speeds up to 200 miles (322 km) per hour! It is one of the busiest rail lines in the world. The Shinkansen carries more than 150 million passengers every year.

THE CHUNNEL

In Europe the Channel Tunnel, or "Chunnel," goes under the English Channel to connect England and France. It travels about 24 miles (38.6 km) underwater, which makes it the longest underwater tunnel in the world. The Chunnel is used by both passenger trains and freight trains. Some people even drive their car onto a train car to catch a ride between the two countries.

subway—a system of trains that runs underground in a city

WILD ANIMALS IN THE CITY

COYOTES

In some neighborhoods you may see or hear coyote activity at night. Coyotes prefer to stay out of populated areas. But sometimes they become comfortable around people. They've been known to attack small pets and steal food and garbage. If you see one in your neighborhood, stay away and don't feed it. The coyote needs to be **hazed**. This means that it needs to be taught to fear humans again. Contact the Humane Society to help scare the coyote away.

haze—to make loud noises and scare wild animals away from populated areas

Have you ever taken out the trash and discovered a fat raccoon or opossum sitting on the dumpster? When we think of wild animals, we don't normally think of the city. But cities do have some wildlife living in them. Read on to learn what you should do if you come across a wild animal in your neighborhood.

WILD DOGS

Most stray dogs in the city aren't truly wild animals. But you still need to be careful if you see one. If the dog is scared or sick, it can be dangerous. Take note of its behavior. If the dog is baring its teeth, growling, and acting aggressive—stay away. Call your local animal control service so officials can safely move it.

However, if the dog seems happy and friendly, you can try to return it to its owner. If it's wearing a collar and tags, check for an address and phone number. Call the owners and let them know you found their pet. If there is no collar, take the dog to an animal control service. Officers there may be able to find the dog's owners, or help find a good home for it.

ALLIGATORS

Have you heard stories about alligators living in city sewers? Actually, such stories are just popular **myths**. Alligators are tropical animals. It's too cold in most city sewers for them. But occasionally alligators are seen roaming the streets in cities with warm climates. They can also show up in parks near swampy areas where they live.

If you happen to see one of these powerful reptiles, back away quickly. Try to stay at least 15 feet (4.6 meters) away. Alligators can't run fast for long. But they can cover short distances very quickly. Call animal control so the animal can be moved to a safe location.

If an alligator does manage to get you in its jaws, you need to fight back as hard as you can. The animal will probably try to drag you into nearby water, where you would drown. Hit or poke it in the eyes with something hard. If you can't get at the eyes, go for the animal's nostrils.

RACCOONS AND OPOSSUMS

These animals can live just about anywhere—even in a busy city. They might make their homes in people's garages, attics, or sheds. And they'll eat just about anything, including garbage. Sometimes these animals seem cute, but they can carry disease. Plus, they can be nasty fighters.

To keep them away, don't let them smell food or trash. Get a trashcan with a sealable lid. Keep pet food inside and put away any leftovers. If you see one of these animals coming toward you, back away—especially if they have food or young nearby. They normally don't want anything to do with humans. If you leave them alone, they'll usually leave you alone. But if you see one that continues to cause problems, call your local animal control office to get rid of it.

MIGHTY RAPTORS

Many birds of prey nest in the nooks and window ledges of tall city buildings. Look up and you might see **raptors** circling high above the streets. If you're lucky, you might see a peregrine falcon diving at speeds up to 200 miles (322 km) per hour to snatch its prey! One family of peregrine falcons has nested at Legg Mason tower in Baltimore, Maryland, for many generations. Search the Internet for raptor Webcams, and you can watch these awesome birds in their urban nests.

myth—a false idea that many people believe

raptor—a bird of prey that hunts and eats small animals

GROW A COOL INDOOR PLANT

You don't need to live in the country or have a big garden to grow some cool plants. Plants help add personality to any home, no matter where you live. Here are several interesting plants you can grow in an apartment or other small indoor space.

cactus

CACTUS Some types of cactus are very colorful, and they hardly need any maintenance.

glow-in-the-dark mushrooms

ALOE VERA This plant is easy to grow and cool to look at. Its sap also has healing properties. People often use it to soothe burns.

MUSHROOMS Some edible mushrooms are tasty and loaded with **nutrients**. Others are poisonous and shouldn't be eaten, but all are weird and interesting to look at. Some even glow in the dark! Get some moist soil and a clear bowl or tank. Set it up in a cool dark place and see if you can grow your own glow-in-the-dark fungus!

nutrient—a substance, such as vitamins, that plants and animals need for good health

DWARF FRUIT TREE

You can grow your own fruit right in your living room! Dwarf fruit trees grow only a few feet tall and are easy to care for. Try growing your own apples, oranges, bananas, cherries, or other delicious fruit.

VENUS FLYTRAP

What a cool plant. It not only brings greenery into your home—it also catches bugs!

Venus flytrap

BURP!

dwarf fruit tree

COMMUNITY GARDENS

In cities with little green space, people sometimes work together to grow community gardens. As people grow fruits and vegetables, they often grow closer as a community. People help make their neighborhoods nicer to look at and often become good friends as well. Do an Internet search to see if any community gardens are in your area. If not, maybe you can start one with your neighbors.

VISIT AWESOME CITY BUILDINGS

Cities everywhere have cool or unusual architecture. Take a look around where you live. You might find a funky bridge, a massive old flourmill, or some other weird building. Ask a librarian to help you learn about unique structures where you live. Then go see them in person. Here are some examples of awesome buildings in cities around the world.

THE FOREST SPIRAL

This housing complex in Darmstadt, Germany, opened in 2000. The building rises up in a spiral pattern. Its diagonal roof is covered with grass, trees, and other plants.

architecture—the design of buildings

KANSAS CITY PUBLIC LIBRARY

The Kansas City Public Library in Kansas City, Missouri, looks just like a library shelf lined with giant books. Even the interior is designed to look like you are entering a huge book.

GUGGENHEIM MUSEUM

The Guggenheim Museum in Bilbao, Spain, opened in 1997. The art museum's design features a unique combination of shapes. The building itself is like a work of art.

SYDNEY OPERA HOUSE

The Sydney Opera House opened in 1973 in New South Wales, Australia. It sits on a point of land in Sydney Harbour and is surrounded by water on three sides. With its curved shell roof design, it resembles a large sailing ship sitting on the water.

PLAY COOL NEIGHBORHOOD SPORTS

DISC GOLF

You can play this game alone, but it's more fun with a few friends. Each player needs a flying disc, such as a Frisbee. Choose a starting point, such as someone's front steps. Then choose your first target, or "hole," to hit with the discs. The target can be a tree trunk, bike rack, tire swing, or anything else that won't be damaged easily.

Each player takes a turn at the starting point throwing his disc toward the target. The players then find their discs and keep taking turns until they each hit the target. Keep track of each player's **strokes** as you play. Then pick a new target and repeat the process. A full game includes nine holes. At the end of the ninth hole, the player with the lowest score wins.

STOOPBALL

This is another classic game that's perfect for guys who want to play baseball but don't have much space. You'll need a quiet side street with little to no traffic. You'll also need two teams of two or three players, a tennis ball or other bouncy rubber ball, and a **stoop**.

1. One player begins as the batter. The player stands in the street by the curb and faces the stoop. His teammates and the other team spread out behind him.

2. The batter starts by throwing the ball hard against the stoop. The goal is to bounce the ball back onto the street as many times as possible. If the ball bounces on the sidewalk, it's a strike. After three strikes, the batter is out.

3. If the ball bounces in the street once, it's a single. An imaginary runner, called a ghost runner, goes to first base. If the ball bounces twice, it's a double and ghost runners advance two bases. Three bounces are a triple and four bounces count as a home run. Every time a ghost runner gets to home plate, the batting team scores a point.

4. If a player on the other team catches the ball before it bounces in the street, it's an out. After three outs, the teams switch sides.

TIP: Use neighborhood objects such as mailboxes or benches to set foul lines for the game.

stroke—a golf term meaning the swing of a golf club; in disc golf a stroke counts as a throw of the disc

stoop—a porch with steps in front of a house or other building

AWESOME FREE THINGS TO DO IN A CITY

Are you short on cash? No worries! One of the great things about cities is that there are tons of awesome free things to do. Try out the following ideas, and then take a look around your city. You'll probably find hundreds of other cool free things you can do.

1. **TOUR HISTORICAL SITES.** Every city has its own unique history. Ask your librarian to help you learn about the history in your city. Then visit the places where important events have happened.

2. **TOUR CITY SERVICES.** Your city probably has water treatment plants, public transportation centers, and other places that the public can tour. It's a great way to learn how your city works.

3. **VISIT A LIBRARY.** The world is at your fingertips at the library. From classic books to the Internet, libraries are great places to let your imagination soar.

4. **VISIT A MUSEUM.** Most cities have museums or art galleries filled with incredible artifacts and artwork. Some of these places are completely free. Many others have certain days that are free and open to the public.

5. **GO TO A PARK.** You may not have a big backyard, but most cities do an awesome job of creating parks and other public outdoor spaces. Nature is also good for your mood—and your brain! Studies show that spending time in nature increases your ability to focus.

6. VOLUNTEER TO HELP. There are dozens of ways you can help in your community. You can help clean up a park or other public space. You can offer to help do chores for the elderly. Or you can ask how you can help at a local charity or an animal shelter.

7. GO GEOCACHING. People often think this outdoor treasure-hunting game is only done in the wilderness. But it can take place in cities too. Do some research online about geocaching in your area. You can use a **Global Positioning System** (GPS) device if you have one. Or just print out a map and follow clues to find treasures hidden near you.

8. VISIT PUBLIC ART AND ART FESTIVALS. Many cities have a variety of public statues, sculptures, and artwork that anyone can go see. Search your city's website to learn where they are located. You can also check out any free art festivals that may be held in your city.

9. WALK OR BIKE. Learn about your city while getting some exercise at the same time. Cities often feature interesting hiking and biking trails, and some cities offer awesome walking tours.

CITY FESTIVALS

Many large cities hold festivals that are an important part of their history and culture. For example, Carnival takes place every year in Rio de Janeiro, Brazil. And New Orleans, Louisiana, is well known for its Mardi Gras festival. At these celebrations thousands of people enjoy parades, lively music, colorful costumes, and a lot of delicious food.

Carnival parade in Rio de Janeiro

Global Positioning System—an electronic device used to find the location of an object

WHICH CITY WAS SCARIEST?

Throughout history, life in big cities has often been gross and dangerous.

Even modern cities can have their share of disease and pollution. Which of these historical cities would you be the most scared to live in?

ANCIENT ROME

MEDIEVAL LONDON

	ANCIENT ROME	MEDIEVAL LONDON
CRIME	Ancient Rome was a dangerous place. The city couldn't afford police officers. Thieves and violent gangs roamed the streets at all hours.	During the Middle Ages (about 400-1500), violent crime was common. Criminals often went unpunished. But if they were caught, punishment was severe. The bodies of hanged criminals were often left on display for weeks as a warning to other lawbreakers.
HEALTH	Most Roman people were slaves or very poor. They usually lived in crowded, filthy apartments. Their food was often filled with parasites. People suffered from terrible diseases, such as malaria and typhoid. Even worse, both sick and healthy people commonly bathed together in public baths, which just helped spread disease.	People didn't know about germs hundreds of years ago. Many thought disease spread through bad smells or bad luck. In the mid-1300s, bubonic plague killed tens of millions of people worldwide. So many died that the dead had to be buried in mass graves.
GROSS FACT	Instead of using bathrooms, poor Romans relieved themselves in chamber pots. In the morning they would dump the pots out the window into the street. Look out below!	Many doctors thought sicknesses came from evil spirits. They sometimes cut holes in patients' skulls to let the bad spirits "bleed out." Not surprisingly, few patients survived this "cure."

FACT:

In the Middle Ages, many barbers did more than just cut hair. They performed surgeries and dental work on people too! The red-and-white striped pole outside their shops symbolized the work they did. The red stripes stood for blood, and the white stripes stood for bandages.

parasite—an animal or plant that lives on or inside another animal or plant
bubonic plague—a deadly disease that causes high fevers, painful swelling of the lymph glands, and darkening of the skin; during the Middle Ages the plague was quickly spread by fleas that lived on rats

INCREDIBLE CITY RECORDS

FIRST CHEESEBURGER

PASADENA, California, was home to Lionel Sternberger. In 1924 he reportedly became the first person to slap a slice of cheese on a burger. Thanks for the awesome sandwich, Lionel!

LARGEST POPULATION

When comparing individual cities, **SHANGHAI**, China, easily has the biggest population in the world. Nearly 18 million people live inside Shanghai's city limits. However, look beyond the main city to include the **suburbs**, and Shanghai drops out of the top 10. The city with the largest metro area population is **TOKYO**, Japan, with about 32 million people.

MOST SPORTS CHAMPIONSHIPS

NEW YORK CITY boasts the most sports championships of any city in the world. The city's baseball, basketball, football, and hockey teams have claimed a total of 55 championship titles.

BIGGEST ROCK STARS

LIVERPOOL, England, was home to the Beatles. The Beatles have sold more albums than any other band in history.

MOST U.S. PRESIDENTS

The **CHARLOTTESVILLE**, Virginia, area has supplied the most U.S. presidents. Thomas Jefferson, James Madison, and James Monroe were all born in or near Charlottesville.

TALLEST BUILDING

The city of **DUBAI**, United Arab Emirates, claims the world's tallest building. The Burj Khalifa skyscraper opened in January 2010 and is 2,722 feet (830 meters) tall. That's more than half a mile high!

MOST AMUSEMENT PARK VISITORS

LAKE BUENA VISTA, Florida, has only 10 permanent residents. However, it is home to Disney World's Magic Kingdom theme park and Typhoon Lagoon water park. Nearly 17.5 million people visit the Magic Kingdom each year, and more than 2 million people visit Typhoon Lagoon.

MOST MULTI-MILLIONAIRES

LONDON, England, is home to 4,224 multi-millionaires. The city also hosts the second most tourists in the world. Almost 17 million people visited London in 2012.

---

suburb—a community immediately outside of city limits

GLOSSARY

architecture (AR-kuh-tek-chuhr)—the design of buildings

bubonic plague (boo-BON-ik PLAYG)—a deadly disease that causes high fevers, painful swelling of the lymph glands, and darkening of the skin; during the Middle Ages the plague was quickly spread by fleas that lived on rats

geocache (GEE-oh-cash)—an outdoor treasure-hunting game; people hide containers with "treasures" inside for others to find

Global Positioning System (GLOH-buhl puh-ZI-shuh-ning SISS-tuhm)—an electronic device used to find the location of an object

haze (HAYZ)—to make loud noises and scare wild animals away from populated areas

myth (MITH)—a false idea that many people believe

nutrient (NOO-tree-uhnt)—a substance, such as vitamins, that plants and animals need for good health

parasite (PAIR-uh-site)—an animal or plant that lives on or inside another animal or plant

raptor (RAP-tohr)—a bird of prey that hunts and eats small animals

stoop (STOOP)—a porch with steps in front of a house or other building

stroke (STROHK)—a golf term meaning the swing of a golf club; in disc golf a stroke counts as a throw of the disc

suburb (SUH-buhrb)—a community immediately outside of city limits

subway (SUHB-way)—a system of trains that runs underground in a city

READ MORE

Bell-Rehwoldt, Sheri. *The Kids' Guide to Classic Games.* Kids' Guides. North Mankato, Minn.: Capstone Press, 2009.

Graham, Ian. *Megastructures: Tallest, Longest, Biggest, Deepest.* Buffalo, N.Y.: Firefly Books, 2012.

Steele, Phillip. *City.* DK Eyewitness Books. New York: DK Publishing, 2011.

INTERNET SITES

FactHound offers a safe, fun way to find Internet sites related to this book. All of the sites on FactHound have been researched by our staff.

Here's all you do:

Visit www.facthound.com

Type in this code: 9781476539232

Check out projects, games and lots more at
www.capstonekids.com

INDEX